AS I WALK

An Inspirational Journey

Edna Beech

As I Walk

Copyright © 2019 by Edna Beech

All rights reserved. No part of this book may be reproduced or transmitted in ANY form or by ANY means without written permission from the author. Any reproduction will is considered criminal and will be punishable to the fullest extent of the law.

Dedication

Inspiration comes in many facets. It comes from above and below. From relationships past and present that have touched us in one way or another. It comes from surroundings of people, places and even something as tiny as the warmth of a child. Even something as insignificant as a falling leaf. Whatever inspires you, grab hold of it and use it as your driving force to keep you motivated and on track.

I've been blessed to have some of the most wonderful people to inspire and motivate me. I want to thank my family, my daughter Kia who brings so much joy to my life; and a special thanks to my sisters who are always there for me. May each of you continue to surround me with the love and comfort we've shared over the years.

Love Always

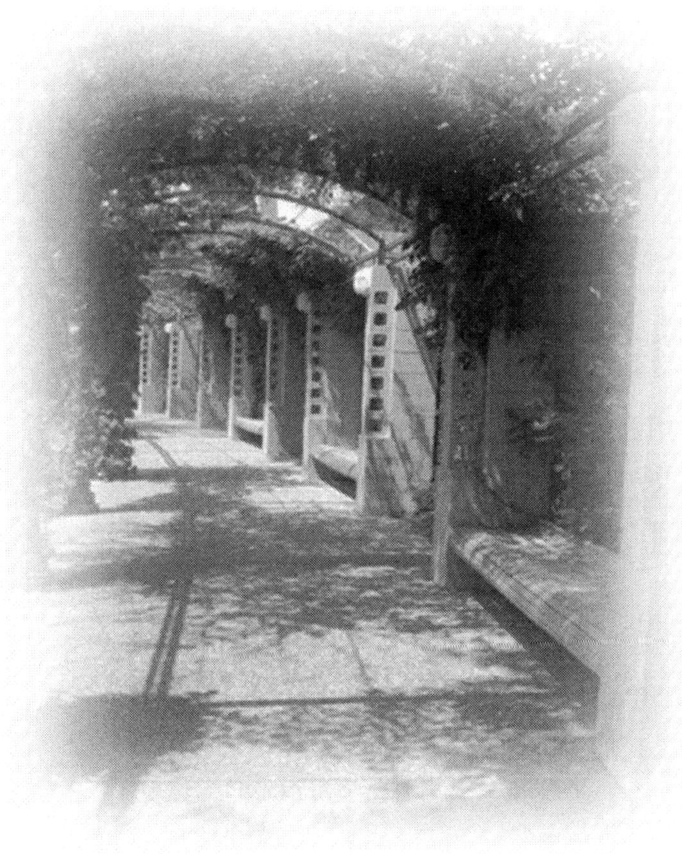

Table of Contents

Self Inventory	8
Trust in Him	13
I'm Here For You	16
Thanksgiving	20
The Beauty I See	25
A Moment In Life	29
All Suited Up	32
All That We Are	36
Love Is	40
Just Passing Through	44
Life's Challenges	49
This Peace I have	52
My Friend	56
Deep Within	61
A Heavy Load	64
Shades of Life	69
On This Day	72
Be Encouraged	77
Someone Special	81
Don't Give Up	84
Because of You	89
Only The Strong	92
My Light	96
Broken – Not Beaten	100
Making Life Count	104
No Time For You	108
Here For You	112
This Is Not Your Fight	116
The One	121
The Dash	124
On Which I Stand	129
Giving Thanks	133
The Price of Freedom	137
The Cross	140
From Beginning To End	144

Self Inventory

How did I get here
I've searched myself but the answer is nowhere
near
Could it be I've fallen from grace
And into the wrong place
I once walked with Him
Instead I'm now in the midst of darkness and
the light is dim

I find it difficult to move ahead
Without feeling loneliness and dread
My mind is cluttered with weighted thoughts
This is what loss of faith has bought
I was once confident and free
Now I've been brought to one knee
The belief system I had before
Is no more

How do I redeem myself so I can hear his voice
again
This I think requires a master plan
First, I'll pray for forgiveness
And ask to be relieved of this mess
Next I'll repent while I confess
Then pray that my sins are forgiven
Asking for restoration of faithfulness

Once I've done those things
I'll wait for my eagle's wings
For then I'll know I'm back on the path to hear his voice
Listening for his words; not my choice
Only then am I able to soar above this place
And enter into God's sustaining grace

"We lose track of what's important to us and somehow forget how great God truly is. Always know that we're in control of our destiny as we keep him in the forefront and He will guide us on our journey."

Lord, let me be pleasing to you in everything I do. Let every word I speak, my actions and my thoughts be a testimony of how you want me to live.

Trust in Him

When you're hurt more than the world could
ever know
And the tears have begun to flow
God knows your pain
All that you've endured will never surface again
Once you release and let go of this burden
The Lord will see that you stop hurting

All that you've carried up to this day
Will soon be swept away
He is the source of your strength and peace
His joy you will find after this release
Hold your head high my friend
For this is a battle you will surely win

You may not know how or when
But you will surely see victory in the end
The paths we must take are never known
But God gives us the strength to move on
Keep your thoughts free to receive his plan
That only he can give; far greater than any man

"In all you do, know that He's there for you. Trust and believe that He's your true source to get through anything you're faced with."

Father, let your presence surround me and keep me in perfect peace. My thoughts are clear. My heart is open to receive instructions from you.

I'm Here For You

It's been a while since I've written this way
But know that today is a special day
Your spirit may be a bit low
So low that tears have begun to flow
Know that prayer is what it's going to take
To get you through sleep and help you to wake

We're all faced with challenges; some more than others
That's when we turn to friends, sisters and brothers
We help each other through tough times
Lord only knows I've had mine
We weren't born tough
That's why when life gets rough

Faith and belief is what we rely on
To sooth our troubled hearts until each problem is gone
Our minds may be cluttered and we wonder what to do
But God gives us answers by way of scriptures and everything is made anew

Lift up your head and ask Him to guide your life right now
You're not alone so don't make this hard; just ask Him how
Sometimes we think no one understands what we're facing or no one knows how much it hurts
By sharing that experience you'll find that someone else has already been there and worn the same shirts

You never know what others are holding inside from the past
Perhaps those times have given them the strength they needed to last
They're able to reach out when someone is hurting the same way
So God put them here to help you on this day

Open up and you will see
That I'm here for you like HE was for me
Believe in yourself and pray for guidance from the one above
He will give you strength, peace and so much love
He alone will make you strong
Then you can soar high with the eagles where you belong

"Ask for the right words to speak if you're unsure of what to say. Never speak out of anger because usually you say what you've been holding on to. You can't return words spoken to where they came from. What's in your heart will surely come to surface. So... let your heart be filled with love, truth and kindness."

Let me hear from you today Lord so that I can make decisions that line up with your word.

Thanksgiving

Today is a day for thanksgiving and gratitude
We gather with love; void of attitude
We have so much to give thanks for
Many challenges have threatened to rip us apart
We were able to head them off from the start

Our strength and faith kept us grounded
From a distance the band of triumph sounded
War came
We endured just the same
Pain surrounded some
But time soothed that wound and allowed us to move on

Challenges were before us all
Love kept us strong so we wouldn't fall
Fear crept in
Yet we didn't bend
We've always been a strong unit taking each day in stride
Unyielding to negativity holding on to our pride

Our differences are what make each of us who we are
Yet we feed off that to make us shine like a star
The support we lend
Keeps us strong; running on to the end
The challenges we face are easier to bear
Knowing we're not alone because someone else cares

Where we've come from makes us who we are
Our parents are the reason we've gotten this far
We hold strong to each other's hands
When facing battles; not knowing where we'll land
There are those who couldn't be with us today
But we love them anyway

Others who were unable to make it here
Our prayers are with them be it far or near
For we have much to be thankful for this year
As we part from this day
And each goes their separate way

Let us continue to reach out to one another throughout the year
We're blessed with phones, cars and voices to hear
Day after day we need to feel the other's presence and know it's there
Let us continue to reach out and show how much we care

Leave YOUR mark with each step you take. YOUR footsteps are the signature of YOUR presence here. Make a difference on YOUR journey through life.

Choose a Path that leads to something that makes a difference in your life.

Lord, place my feet on the path you want me to go and let the Holy Spirit continue to be with me every step of the way.

The Beauty I See

You've blossomed into more than I could ever hope for
And I know there's far more in store
The things you will see
No one can tell you what they'll be
The things you'll do
No one will know but you

Where you will go
Pray before you leave and a path He will show
There are many roads before you
Some obvious, some not so plainly set in view
A beautiful young lady is what I see before me today
From the tiny infant that warmed my heart in every way

Your eyes hold visions that others will never know
They've watched and witnessed people come and go
Ears have heard many facts to guide over time
Listening and gathering what's necessary for God's light to shine

Lips that speak wisdom beyond your years
To comfort those in need while shedding tears
Continue to shine like the glorious light you are
You are my inspiration and my brightest star

"I'm watching you grow each day. You'll never know how very proud of you I am. Keep God in your life and allow him to lead your steps. He's always watching you and allowing you to grow into the person you're destined to become."

Give me the strength today Lord to keep on moving in the direction you want me to go. Keep my heart, mind and eyes focused on you always.

A Moment In Life

Today is a precious gift
The Creator has smiled upon us once again
We dispel all hurt and pain
As we move forward
With truth and with honor we continue our journey
Seeking to find higher grounds
And life's yearning

Those forces that were once against us
Are no longer a threat or a thought
Because our destiny has already been bought
We give no countenance to the negativity
That once plagued our minds and our bodies
This keeps us down and in captivity

With peace and with love
We are brought to the next road we must travel
Our steps are not our own
And where we'll end up is not known
We know not what is expected
Or at best what we should be
But we know our life is far from being complete

We will win each challenge or defeat
As one by one they unfold
We have no worries and have no cares
No time for sorrows or tears
The gift we've been given is so unbelievable
How can we keep it all and not share
It is by far the most precious thing we'll ever get
So let's live each day with no regret

"We take for granted the days we're given and waste away the nights. Each day is truly a gift that should be opened carefully and cherished to the fullest. Never let the day end without showing appreciation for this gift called life."

Stay close Father and renew my peace each day. Allow me always to rely on you as my strength when I feel weak.

All Suited Up

I awakened today the same as the day before
Only this time it wasn't a chore
I got of bed with comfort and ease
Rose with a smile from the rustling of nearby trees
I gave thanks for yet another day
And prayed that God will continue to show me the way

I got dressed; put on my suit of armor
Braced myself and headed for the door
Whatever lied ahead
I knew couldn't touch my head
Any debris covering the street
Would never touch my feet

Any cloud forming in the sky
Wouldn't be allowed to darken my eye
All manner of germs on this land
Wouldn't come in contact with my hand
Any negative chatter that may be near
Wouldn't stand a chance of reaching my ear
All forces of evil that may exist
Would be rushed away with a flick or twist

Any worries or fear that are about to start
Would never penetrate my heart
Feelings of jealousy, shame or doubt may erupt
But they'll never fill my cup
Words of anger may tempt me to slip
But they won't escape from my lips
For I declare this a good day
I walk proud and strong; a child of God on display

"Starting the day with a little inspiration is just what we need to get moving in the right direction. Just keep meditating on something positive to remain rooted to assure your day goes well."

You were created for greatness. Let your light shine bright today so that everyone can see who you really are.

All That We Are

Life isn't always what it seems
It's filled with hopes and dreams
It comes with good and bad
From experiences we've had
It comes with ups and downs
With smiles and frowns

It comes with disappointments and setbacks
Sometimes in small packages; sometimes piles and stacks
It comes with clouds of rain
And with tears and pain
These things are a part of the picture
One that makes us stronger and richer

It's there to show us the way
Making us the people we are to become someday
Once the clouds are removed and the sun comes out
We forget about those times when we were down and could not shout
Lifted up so high
Able to view earth's creation and a cloud filled sky

In life we all must bend to circumstances
It's how we rise that determines how our life enhances
A new beginning is given to us each day
The chance to see God's vibrant colors or view life as gray
We must grow and reach for higher ground
Putting negativity on mute blocking out the sound

Surrounding ourselves with positive energy and creative thoughts
Realizing the road ahead is far greater than where we've been brought
This message has been created
Through visions and words that have been stated

Someone very close helped me to see
How important life is to me
Through his words and all the love he's shown
I am able to express how much I've grown
I share with you today these words of Inspiration
Hoping they will reach, touch and love away all frustration

"Strive for greatness, live for peace and happiness. Ask God every day for wisdom to make the right decisions. Let those decisions make a difference every day you're here."

Thought of the Day

My joy is in knowing you're there no matter where I find myself.

Love Is

You asked what love is to me
Well I think I can speak openly and freely
To you I will bear my soul
Cause the truth has to be told
Love has been revealed to me over time
Now just let me speak my mind

It's none of these superficial definitions or play on words
No my friend that's for the birds
The greatest gift of all is to love and be loved in return
And in doing so many have gotten burned
Yet GOD so love the world that he gave his only begotten son

I believe this is the ultimate love; second to none
To love is to commit willingly
To give of yourself unconditionally
With a feeling of wanting nothing in return
For this is something we all must learn
Seeing the beauty in that particular person or thing
A joy that no other can bring

A bond or connection that only you two share
Like a particular look or stare
Love is the deepest feeling you can have for another
It's shared with more than your father or mother
Yet so confused with other emotions and desires
It's used as an excuse to quench fires

Longing, desire, lust and wanting; just to name a few
Yes I'm sure they've tricked you too
To say I love you is a feeling that's true
It's what I share openly when I give myself to you
But to give me you and take all of me
Is my idea of a love that's free

Pouring it out into a bottomless heart
Accepting and appreciating is understood from the start
As we embark on this brave new quest to know love
We first have to love the one above
This is my idea of what love is to me
It's the highest of highs
And deeper than any sea

"It's so easy to be angry with a loved one. We walk around every day holding on to little things that someone did or said to anger us. How then can you say you're happy and have peace in your heart? Forgiveness is the key to all happiness. Let go of the lie and live in truth so that you can have happiness and true peace."

Deliver me Lord from fear and let me rest in your bosom of comfort and assurance. There I find my way and know that you are with me no matter what I face.

Just Passing Thru

Caught up you say
I'll catch you another day
Don't call because I'm too busy for you
You have no idea what I have to do
Activities of life are weighing me down
Running me all around town

Hours quickly turn into a week; and then
We start all over again
Where does time go
The hustle of life has ceased human kindness
to grow
At what point do we stop or slow the pace
Just long enough to say thanks, hello or to say
grace

The simplest things are creating irritation
Causing one to snap out of mere frustration
The people we love and should hold close
We've pushed far away, yet we need them
most
Always on the go and moving fast
How long can our existence last

We're so engulfed in our own personal challenges
Not seeing how life is displaced or so unbalanced
Afraid of ridicule, gossip or what others may say
We hold inside any guilt, hurt or pain and that's where it'll stay
We take for granted and don't think twice

About this precious gift called life
It was given to us along with tools to use
But we do with it as we choose
We were created for a far greater cause
Yet we can't take a moment just to pause
We're here only for a short time
Take a break from the flow and relax your mind

"So much going on in life that we just don't have time for the simplest things in life... keeping in touch or reaching out to one another. Make time to share your life with those you care about. Cherish the moments and hold each and every day dear to your heart. "

I am inspired by your presence that surrounds me no matter where I find myself or what comes my way.

Life's Challenges

We are challenged from all facets of life
Constantly hit with stress and strife
Some bend, some break
As we declare this is all we can take

Yet to reach deep inside to find the strength within
Is how we fight all battles we're in
Letting courage take form
Relying on faith to move on
We cannot be ruled by yesterday's troubles
Because tomorrow's may be tripled or doubled

Instead we look beyond for what's to come
Pushing aside thoughts of feeling glum
Assurance is a testimony given from the one above
Holding on to his unconditional love

He offers peace when we need it most
That stretches beyond any coast
His hand is there so hold on tight
Turning all situations around; setting things right
No matter where you are or what you do
Just know He is always there for you

"Life has a way of presenting distractions on a daily basis; but God gives us the strength to handle them. Courage and faith are a constant source to keep us focused."

Today Lord, I will rise high knowing you have given me the power I need to succeed.

This Peace I Have

A stillness enfolds and keeps me still
I take my time doing his will
It wraps me in its warm embrace
Holding me as I seek his face
Removing the cares of the world from my path
Because each day presents a different wrath

Carefully I listen for his calling
As if someone is holding and keeping me from falling
A warmth that fulfills my total being
No one sees or knows what I'm feeling
A light that shines to guide my way
As I trust it gets simpler each day

Coolness when things heat up
Without expectations he fills my cup
He has Love that has no end
It's as soft as a breeze from the gentlest wind
A breath of fresh air that you can't resist inhaling
He's there always to keep me from failing

He's there with me in my thoughts and dreams
Through valleys, brooks and streams
Guiding my steps and leading me in the
directions I must go
There for me in ways I don't even know

I'm thankful for his presence and for this peace
within
This praise I have will never end
He's given me so much that I have to share
I'm so filled with emotions beyond compare

"I could never thank you enough for all that you are and all that you do. Every moment of the day or night you're where I can find you."

Allow me to dwell in your secret place Lord where I can feel your presence. Here is where I can seek and find you.

My Friend

I have to tell about someone I've met
Because he's going to be hard to forget
This person is kind and sweet
One who's touched my heart significantly
His sincerity reached out and touched an inner place
For he could see the wounds not shown on my face

Cast out all your cares he said
As he looked sideways and nodded his head
Worry not for the *Lord* is here
If you want to talk I'm always near
I have a pretty good ear and I listen well
Call me up if you have a story to tell

Stop to see me if you're close by
Just for conversation or to say hi
Our time at this location is drawing to a close
He said as he twitched his nose
But I'm only a phone call away
If you have something to say

This is the person I've come to know
The one behind the warm smile and inner glow
Continue reading further on
Perhaps you'll understand how this friendship will live even though I'm gone

This is just a brief overview
Of what I see in you
A calming spirit that touches your heart
One that captures you from the very start
Gifted with words that sooth your troubles away
Speaking your point directly with no hesitation
or delay

A quote from the scriptures that's right on
queue
Allowing one to see you point of view
As if placed here for a special reason
To guide and help mend for a time or season
You my friend are a rare find
As you go forward; leaving us behind

Keep in touch for I hate to lose the friend I've
found
It's going to be difficult not having you around
I've come to enjoy my short visits with you
You're a treasure in this chest of people
One that's honest and true

"What we say is just as important as what we do. Our words are what people hear that reach ears and pierce hearts. Our actions are seen and create memorable images that leave lasting impressions. Lets make sure our words and actions are expressions of love and sincerety."

Pour out your blessings upon me this day Lord that I may fulfill the purposes you have established for my life.

Deep Within

Inside myself I find comfort
Here's where everything about life I can distort
When hurt comes my way
I pretend I'm okay
When I feel down
No one can get past my frown

When problems arise
My smile is used as a disguise
Whatever I'm going through
Is buried deep and from everything I withdrew
Current issues and past
Are crushing me and I'm drowning fast
I don't know how I'm going to last

Someone said to pray and ask for peace
That this will give me some relief
They said cast your cares on Him
But I don't know how to release them
They tried to convince me to step out on faith
It will ease my pain and this heavy weight

They said to lean not on my understanding or mans
But to trust in the Lord and wait for his plans
To know that this life is not my own
But everything is from the seeds we've sown
We must live not inside ourselves or as one
Or to suffer the sins and wrongs we've done

"Do you ever think about how wonderful life really is? We have so much to be thankful for. So much we can do each day to make a great impact on someone's life. Let's live it with a purpose that leaves a positive memory for those we touch."

I am marveled by the glory of your handiwork as I look upon each day viewing all your creations.

A Heavy Load

As I walk this lonely road called life
I carry with me years of strife
Days of hurt have consumed my thoughts
And robbed me of everything I bought
I think constantly of the tracks I took
And the decisions that lead to this dry brook

The pain I caused others along the way
Is on my mind each day
The lies I told
Have gripped my heart and finally taken hold
All the deception I've used
For the game were mere tools

The webs I've weaved to get into others lives
Are coming back on me as outbreak of hives
All the tears shed because of me
Is holding me in captivity
It's a constant reminder of what I am
And how I just didn't give a damn

I realize each act has repercussions I must face
Before I leave this place
I must pay the toll to get through the gate
A coin for each and every mistake
Change is inevitable so search your heart
For this is where you must start

Much forgiveness is needed for the peace you
seek
Honesty and sincerity will also help to defeat
This battle you wish to win
Prayer is the sword you'll use to destroy
lifelong sins

"People say let it go, or you don't know how much I've been hurt or how bad things are. That could all be true. What matters is what you do during those times. This is what truly determines the outcome."

Each day is a new beginning to make a difference not just for ourselves but to others. Let those around you know that you care.

Shades of Life

I see life in shades of colors
It has a way of displaying others
Every walk of life is viewed
Patches here and there are glued
It reminds me of a scrapbook
That illustrates the roads we took

It brings us to where we are today
And reveals where we've been and the roles
we play
It leaves traces of hidden talents and battle
scars
Paths taken and the distance gone and how far
We're left with memories of yesteryear
And long for glimpses of the past that bring
about a tear

Everything we do is etched in our past
Images and shapes in a vivid contrast
Each color represents a phase
Some crystal clear; others just a haze
It creates a bond that keep memories clear
To share with those who are dear

As generations evolve and families grow
We pass on the yesteryears of what we know
This creates the patchwork we've made
Along the way and the foundations we've laid

"We're all connected in one way or another. Life allows us to build lasting relationships. We nurture them and allow them to create lasting memories throughout the years."

Prepare a way for me Lord that I may walk according to your will and follow your word.

On This Day

I hold fast to hope
That our neighborhoods aren't plagued with dope
That the streets our children walk and play on
Are safe from some thug carrying a gun
That our mothers and fathers
Are free from thieves and robbers

And all that we've worked so hard to acquire
Isn't taken by a crack head that need a fix to get a little higher
That we're able to speak intelligently with one another
Before our language is destroyed any further
That our people will get up and improve the situation they're in
By taking the time right now to figure out where to begin

People fought and died for justice in hopes that we'll learn to love each other
Yet we'll lie, cheat and sell each other out just to get a step further
We settle for little and hope for less
And give up when we're put to the test

Our lives are valuable but it's hard to tell
From looking at the destruction, hatred and lifestyles leading us straight to hell
How much more must we endure
Before realizing there's already a cure

As darkness unfolds its great plan
To engulf us in poverty and enslave man
We only have this time to reverse the damage done
Only then will we have victory and declare this battle won

"Hope is something we can always rely on to give us what we need to keep on moving forward. We need one another to get through life. Stay close and uplift each other."

Streams of living water shall pour out upon me each day to cleanse my life and purify my heart. I will rejoice as I go about the day knowing I am transformed.

Be Encouraged

Before you fall asleep
Think about what you want to keep
Hold on tight
To those things that give you strength to take flight

Keep close to you
All you know that's honest and true
Be willing to give
To get closer to how you want to live
Each step you make
Will bring you closer to the road you must take

Be not afraid of what's to come
God will give you all the tools you need
To mold you into what you'll become
You'll rise higher than you ever thought you could
And uprooted from where you once stood

Only to find yourself where you never though you could be
So keep your chin up
Because everything you endure will only become a memory

"As you go through life and encounter obstacles from day to day, remain prayerful and surround yourself with positivity. Always remember that it's only temporary. Continue to stay encouraged no matter what you see or think."

Give me the words to speak Lord that I may help someone who needs to hear from you. Empower me with your word so that it flows sweetly from my lips.

Someone Special

There are those who are born for a special reason
Then there are some who are here for a season
Some come to touch our lives in a special way
Others are here just for a day
Many come to lift our spirits and share the gift of love
That shines through us from above

Every once in a while we meet some who encompass it all
Someone who is neither great nor small
Yet what they share warms your heart
And make you feel so special from the very start
You are one that possess all these things
And you've touched people with words as soft as an angel's wings

On this day I'd like to say…
May God continue to bless and keep you near
And your words of kindness will forever be a song to my ear
May your goodness shine as bright as the morning sunrise
And the joy one feels in your presence bring our lows to highs

Thanks for the words of kindness that time will never erase
And for bringing a smile to my face
May your memory continue to touch each and every one of us as we live
And the warmth you share remind us daily of the love you give

"Sometimes in life we find that special someone that makes life complete. One that makes you feel you can accomplish anything as your friendship blossoms. Stay close as you embrace each day and let nothing come between you."

Dwell within me Lord so that I may be a better person each day. Give me the ability to shine brightly because your light lives within me.

Don't Give Up

How can I say what I feel today
To express how you make me feel this way
From the beating of my heart to a love song
You've captured my heart, my love and what
we share is strong

Each day I feel you near
Even though sometimes I long for your and
shed a tear
But you're in my heart and there you will stay
No matter what challenges we face or the roles
we play
If we stand strong together
We can handle any weather

When you truly love someone
Life is good through bad times or while having
fun
When you reach a little bump in the road
It's there to help reach the next phase that will
unfold
Should we take this and grow
Or do we back up and take it slow

Will we accept our love as another win
A blessing that's been given for us to begin
Again and again and again until we perfect this thing
Because each day we will have something new that life will bring
But to conquer each battle and put it to rest
Is all about life, love and living each and every moment to its best

"A lot of the times we feel like giving up when life seems to be wearing us down. That's when we need Him the most. Stay encouraged and let your thoughts be centered on what you know to be honest and true."

Allow me to come in contact with those who are able to help fulfill today's purpose Lord. Remove all negativity from my thoughts and presence.

Because of You

All that I am I owe to you
Because it's you who walk me through
For being there through all the tough times
And helping to ease my mind
You're up with me at night
When I'm battling wrong and right

You smooth the roads ahead
Guide through places where I'm led
There with me all during the day
Keeping me sane encouraging me to pray
Fighting off the wolves when they get too close
This is when I need you the most

Placing your hedge of comfort all around me
Giving me protection that no one else can see
You lift my spirits when they're low
And give me courage when fear starts to show

You're always behind me giving me that little push
Keeping me at a steady pace so I'm careful not to rush
You are my strength that will always lead my life
That keeps me in peace; void of all strife

"Every step we make leads us to the path we should take. Sometimes we venture off that path and lose track of where we're headed. Keep your thoughts clear and listen closely and He will lead the way."

My actions today will be reflective of the person that I am, not what I was or what anyone thinks I am. Because my savior made me a magnificent specimen, I believe I can walk with my head held high and do anything I set out to do.

Only The Strong

I thought of you today
No particular reason I'd say
Memories of you marched across my mind
I kept on working, trying to put them behind
But they kept on coming, weighing on my heart
Each one captured me; where do I start

First there was your strength
Something most have but not to your extent
Then there's your patience
A quality that's unique and sometimes non-existent
Next we have endurance
A gift, a blessing that's assurance

Then there's the love you exhibit
And your willingness to give
Which is shown by the way you live
You've endured so much for all
Yet still stand tall

Faced many trials on your race
With no jury judge or lawyer to plead your case
Walked alone through darkness and pain
And found your way out without a stain
Carried heavy burdens on such small shoulders
Possibly as heavy as a boulder

Throughout these times and times of old
Know that you are an everlasting stronghold
The light we will see and remember for years to come
Because your perservence is unknown to some
The person I see before me shines so bright
You're are a lily, a jewel and this family's light

"Most of us are stronger than we give ourselves credit for. The strength we possess lies deep within. Continue to believe in yourself and let your light shine so others can see who you really are."

Be strong and courageous. Let nothing or no one keep you from accomplishing your goals.

My Light

Father you are my light
Without you I can't win this fight
No other can complete me like you
Or guide me quite the way you do
Each day I'm more astonished than before
Of all the riches you have in store

You fill me with so much love and peace
The kind that never cease
So I look for someone to tell my story
About you and your amazing glory

How each time I'm about to fall
You're there before I can place the call
How every time I think I can't take another step
You're there before I know I need help
How time after time I'm about to take the wrong turn
You're there directing my thoughts so I can continue to learn

What you want me to know
And which way you'd like me to go
You are my high when I'm feeling low
My strength when tears begin to flow

The comfort needed when all else fails
Allowing me to enjoy life and all that it entails
I thank you for all that you will be, all that you are and all that you've been
You've given me peace, assurance and the courage to win over and over again

"Give God the praise he deserves. As you look around, you can see all of his amazing blessings. He is truly worthy of all the praise."

Motivate someone today by sharing your life with them. Let them know they're not alone. Give them the encouragement that's needed. The life you've lived is full of experiences that are meant to be shared. That's why our Father allows us to go through difficulties.

Broken – Not Beaten

Keep your chin up my friend
Know this is not the end
For the tribulations of man are not God's way
And you will surely come out on top one day
Though this may seem as if they've won this fight
Know that God's word will set everything right

Each time one of his lambs are wounded from the enemy's attack
He sends an angel of mercy to restore any lack
He replaces what was once torn down
And puts your feet back on solid ground

When you're feeling as if the enemy has you by the throat
That's the time to know the difference between the sheep and the goat
God guides the sheep and leads them into a place of protection
Because there you'll find peace from every possible conviction

Be strong while this challenge is before you
You'll be lifted up and He'll show you what to do
Every step you take He'll be there to guide the path to take
And provide comfort at night and when you wake

Let no man take your pride or steal your joy
You have the endurance to overcome any obstacle or ploy
God gave you strength to carry out his will
And a lifetime of happiness to fulfill

"We're challenged on a daily basis, but I encourage you to stay focused and never give up. Always look up and continue to believe that you can win any battle."

Clear my mind today Lord that I may receive your direction. Let me hear from you so I may follow your precepts. Allow me to receive your plans for my life and follow them as you so direct.

Making Life Count

I heard someone say that it's not what you do
but how
What you've accomplished from the beginning
till now
What you've become
Not where you've come from
Once you're gone you won't know
Where your riches and possessions will go

The lives you've impacted and to what degree
Is what others will remember and discuss
constantly
All the fun and games you've played
Were just filling space for the ground that was
already laid

Life is a day by day expression of what will
once become a memory
Something that those whose lives you've
touched will hold onto dearly
Each day we're blessed with the gift of life
We fill it with garbage, turmoil and strife

We clutter up the greatest thing we've been
given
Some walking around on the brink of death
instead of living
We begin our days with problems from the past
Instead of embracing it with faith; knowing that
all troubles will soon pass

We hold onto unforgiveness when we should
let it go
Yet days, months and even years go by as that
anger continues to grow
Bitterness engulfs us and robs us of our joy
Not realizing that happiness is the one thing it
will destroy

When will we wake up and envelop life as it
was intended to be
With love, understanding, forgiveness, human
kindness and harmony

"When you think about giving in or giving up, that's when it's time to place that call. We have a direct line to a true source who is always waiting to help in our time of need. Always know He's there – any day, any hour, any minute."

You are my peace Lord and I welcome you into my thoughts and my life.

No Time For You

I just have so much to do
Today's activities are pulling me away
Praying can hold off long enough for me to enjoy this day
I'll catch service some other time
Having a life is not a crime

There's a game, movie or party tonight
And my schedule is so tight
I have things I want to do
Lord that don't include you
So many places to go
Giving up two or three hours is more than I can blow

Yet I call on you when things aren't right
But can't find you in the middle of the night
Or when my life is spiraling downhill
And your presence I can't feel
I remember all those times when you weren't first
And it makes me think the worst

What would happen if God was too busy for you
If He had this same attitude too
How would it feel if you knocked on His door
And there was no answer like before
But He's always there any night or day
Behind the scenes making a way

He's there when you're all alone
When everyone else is gone
He's there loving and protecting you always
His mercy endures even if you stray
From the time we wake till we fall asleep He's eternally there
Making provisions and keeping us in his care

"God is always there for us no matter the day or time. We fill our lives with so many activities that we forget to make time for what's truly important."

I am encouraged each and every day to live a better life so that I may help someone along the way.

Here For You

I wasn't sure what to say
To you, my friend on this day
Sometimes we think we understand what someone is going through
But not know the depth of pain that's only within that person's view

I am guilty of trying to help when someone is down or even feeling blue
When it may not be the right thing to do
So, I'll just say this…

Sometimes we carry all the cares and troubles past and present inside
But we're not meant to bear troubles for the mere sake of pride
Continue to share what you feel
Only then can you experience what's real

God is the source of your strength for all you endure
So keep your mind on him and he'll guide you for sure
No matter what your loss or how you feel
He'll give you peace of mind if you'll stay in his will

Remember these thoughts when you start to feel down
And remember, He is there when no one else is around

"Yes we are our brothers' keeper. It's difficult to know what to say or do when we encounter a situation where someone needs our help. Saying or doing the right thing is not always easy. We must always rely on the word and pray for direction when attempting to be there for others in their time of need."

The world is everything you want it to be. Just live life to the fullest each and every day. Get out and enjoy yourself and spend time with those you love.

This is Not Your Fight

Even in your darkest hour
Think of something as simple as a beautiful flower
Or something that brightens your day
That takes all the hurt and pain away
When you believe the worst is happening to you
This is what you should do

Ask God to give you the strength you need
And he will send it with rapid speed
Ask Him to take all that you're going through away in His time
And He will surely ease your mind
Ask Him to give you the gift of peace
And your happiness will slowly increase

Give Him all the troubles you face
And He will wipe them away without a trace
Let Him know every challenge that is in the path you walk
And He will give you the right words to speak when you talk

Tell him all about the enemies surrounding you left and right
He will be your champion for this battle you think you must fight

Renew your faith with Him
And life's light will shine bright where it was once dim
All you have to do is talk to Him about what's going on
He's there waiting for you to pick up the phone

"Many times when we're faced with troubles, we tend to try to resolve them on our own instead of taking it to God for answers. Life will always bring something your way that you're not quite ready for. Next time you're faced with one of life's challenges, take it to God for help."

The path to destiny is already laid from the beginning. Stay focused and ask for direction each day.

The One

You're the reason I get through each day
The only one who makes me feel this way
You are the calm when my life is in turmoil
The one I turn to when there's a storm
You're the love I've always wanted to know

The one that fills me from head to toe
You're the strength when I feel weak
Giving me words when I know not what to speak
You give so much when you should take
The one that keeps me strong when I want to break

You're the light when darkness engulfs me
The one that points the way when I can't see
You're the happiness when I'm sad
And sometimes the good when I'm bad
You allow me to be better than I could ever know
And I'm so thankful that you're the one that makes my heart flow

"I've always longed for a relationship with God that made me feel whole. Or, one where you know without a doubt that you can talk to him about anything and call on him any time. Keep your ear inclined to hear from him. He is always there with open arms."

Seek peace from the moment you open your eyes till you fall asleep. Beware of robbers and thieves for their goal is to steal your job, happiness and livelihood.

Making The Dash

I heard someone say that it's not what you do,
but how
Not what you've done, but here and now
Once you're gone there is no tomorrow
Friends and family are left with grief and sorrow

The lives you've impacted and to what degree
Are filled with a memory
Each day we're blessed with the gift called life
We fill it with garbage, turmoil and strife
We clutter up the greatest thing we've been given
Some walking around on the brink of death
instead of living

We begin the days with remnants of the day
before
Instead of walking through a new open door
Grab hold of every second as if it were your last
Be thankful that it leads to the future; not your
past
Take inventory of every minute of the day
With gratitude that we're given a reprieve to stay

Enjoy all the days you're given because we know
not what will be
Focus your time and energy on the present for
that's all we can see
As each week passes without a trace
Fill it with treasure that nothing can erase
Be thankful for every year that we're given
To know that we're still here to keep on living

We are truly a precious gift that's taken for
granted
Pluck up the weeds that's chocking your life
And water the seeds that are already planted
Unwrap each day to expose all the possibilities
That life has to offer with a sense of ease

"Dwell in a place of peace. We spend so much time focusing on the little things in life. Life was designed for the bigger picture which is selfless. As you go through life, focus on what's important to you."

Let your smile light up someone's life today. Let your words of encouragement spring forward. You can make difference that helps someone feel special.

On Which I Stand

The Rock on which I stand
Is where my feet always tend to land
No matter what happens from month to year
Whether I'm presented with a smile or tear
You're there through my ups and downs
Whether I smile or frown

You're there to comfort me in my hurts and pains
Loving me when there are storms and rains
You guide me through the darkest of times
Helping to ease my mind
You're my strength when I feel weak
My hope when all is bleak

You're the light through the darkest of times
The clarity when I have a troubled mind
You're the love I cherish that nothing can replace
The comfort that fills all space
You are the greatest and no other can compare
I'm comforted knowing you're always there

"You can be comforted knowing that He's always there no matter what is before you. Many times we rely on others and even our own decisions to get us through. Don't hesitate to call on him. He's always waiting to hear from you."

Lift me up today that I may rise higher than the day before. Give me the wisdom and courage I need to overcome any obstacles I may face today.

Giving Thanks

I thank God for sending you
A blessing long overdue
I thank God for this peace we share
For showing me just how much He cares
I thank God for his expressions of love
As sweet as the summer rain; graceful as a dove

I thank God for protection each day
How He keeps enemies at bay
I thank God for guiding my steps
For drying my tears as I wept

I thank God for those little bumps and bruises
For penetrating the mind that I wasn't using
I thank God for those things unforeseen
For delivering me up from thoughts unclean
I thank God for every single breath I take
And for every moment I'm awake

"As we go through life, we live to appreciate those who've been so instrumental in our development. Believe it or not, people are in our lives for a reason. However, everyone wasn't meant to remain in our circle of life. Surround yourself with love, positivity and people who want the best for you."

Let the words you speak today be inspirational as well as motivational. You never know how much a kind word means to someone who's going through something.

The Price of Freedom

The Price of Freedom

Many sacrifices have to be made
To welcome this escapade
Winning battles of this magnitude
Takes a strong will and fortitude

What does one give
And how much should we forgive
We constantly endure daily strife
Knowing this is not God's way of life
Every road to free ourselves has been blocked
Long before the ship was docked

Each day we trudge forward taking baby steps
Yet the enemy has hollowed that path with great depths
He's taken giant leaps to crush any opposition
To enhance his greed; sealing his ambition
From the beginning to the end
He's assured himself of a glorious win

He's stacked from bottom to top
But in the end; on his belly he will flop
Enslaved we were not meant to be
We're equipped with the authority to live free
The system in place will crash and burn

Only then will evil learn
That we have power to discern
And we hold the key
To a kingdom built for eternity

"Trials are inevitable in life. No matter how good we think we are or how close we are to our father, things will happen that we have no control of. Be prayerful and strong while going through. Let your faith be your guiding light. How you handle what you're going through will determine how you come out on the other side."

Family is more than just associatin by blood rights. Get to know each other and about each other. Only then can you truly love and appreciate your family.

The Cross

The heavy burden he carried
Was unknown to Mary
His purpose was revealed to only a few
How it would end, no one knew
Yet God shared a glimpse of this story
Without exposing us to his glory

His existence was all a part of the master plan
His endurance throughout, we could never understand
The thoughts running through his mind
Were undoubtedly overwhelming at that time
Enemies surrounding him on every side
While those professed loyalty lied

Even as they gathered at the last meal
His disciples were still not a hundred percent real
He was tried and convicted of no crime
Yet he'd still have to pay for the life of yours and mine
The penalty according to his accusers
Was to endure punishment by the cruelest abusers

The pain and agony was unbearable as he pressed on
Through the street and up hills while being spit on
Some hissed and called him names
Others wept as they viewed the shame

He was tortured from head to toe
And hung up high as part of the show
Have you thought about the price he paid
Or the role he played
Do you ever wonder about the sacrifice he made
All that we are, all that we have, all that we will become
Are only because of the grounds he laid

"What determines our self worth is not what we have, our jobs or where we live. Who we are inside and how we treat one another is more valuable than any commodity. Live your life to love others each day by sharing yourself, caring for others and giving of yourself."

Nothing can replace life. Seconds, minutes and hours all add up to days as the clock keeps ticking. What you do each day should be meaningful. Don't burden yourself with things you can do nothing about. Never let stress overwhelm you. And let go of things that add no value to your life.

From Beginning to End

After you've done your **B**est and life **C**ontinues to spiral downward; **D**on't give up. **E**ncourage yourself and continue to have **F**aith. **G**ive thanks to God. **H**elp is always nearer than you think. **I**nvite the Holy Spirit to come into your life and **J**esus will always be there for you. **K**eep on praising and **L**iving for His purpose and **M**ake God first in your life. **N**ever give up on yourself. **O**pen your heart to receive his **P**resence. Stop feeling defeated, just keep on pressing forward. **Q**uiet times are where you'll find Him. **R**est in His bosom and know that **S**erenity is where you'll find the peace you seek. **T**rust in Him always. Whenever you get the **U**rge to give up, know that He's always **V**ery close. He's **W**aiting for you to call on Him any day or night. Keep your heart and mind fi**X**ed on Him. **Y**ou will feel Him and know He's near. Incline our ear to hear with **Z**eal. His voice is like a summer breeze that whispers in your ear.

Every journey will leave you with a memory to share. Your life is a compilation of stories that you've lived. This wonderful gift has been given to you for a reason that's not your own. Whatever you've been fortunate enough to witness, share it with others. Whatever you have to say; let your voice be heard. Whatever your talent, share it with as many people as you can come in contact with.

Thank you for your support and love. I pray that every message move you in a special way. I sincerely hope that as you read each word that it penetrates your heart and mind. Be open to receive.

Made in the USA
Columbia, SC
14 June 2023